THE CONSTITUTION AND COMMANDMENTS

Are We Really Founded
on Biblical Principle?

THOMAS N. CULPEPPER

WESTBOW
PRESS®
A DIVISION OF THOMAS NELSON
& ZONDERVAN

Scripture quotations marked HCSB are taken from the Holman
Christian Standard Bible®, Copyright © 1999, 2000, 2002, 2003,
2009 by Holman Bible Publishers. Used by permission. Holman
Christian Standard Bible®, Holman CSB®, and HCSB® are
federally registered trademarks of Holman Bible Publishers.

The Holy Bible, English Standard Version® (ESV®) Copyright © 2001 by
Crossway, a publishing ministry of Good News Publishers. All rights reserved.

Scripture taken from the King James Version of the Bible.

Scripture taken from the American Standard Version of the Bible.

WestBow Press books may be ordered through booksellers or by contacting:

WestBow Press
A Division of Thomas Nelson & Zondervan
1663 Liberty Drive
Bloomington, IN 47403
www.westbowpress.com
1 (866) 928-1240

Because of the dynamic nature of the Internet, any web addresses or
links contained in this book may have changed since publication and
may no longer be valid. The views expressed in this work are solely those
of the author and do not necessarily reflect the views of the publisher,
and the publisher hereby disclaims any responsibility for them.

Any people depicted in stock imagery provided by Thinkstock are models,
and such images are being used for illustrative purposes only.
Certain stock imagery © Thinkstock.

ISBN: 978-1-9736-0610-9 (sc)
ISBN: 978-1-9736-0609-3 (e)

Print information available on the last page.

WestBow Press rev. date: 10/21/2017

Preamble of the Constitution:

"We the people of the United States, in order to form a more perfect Union, establish Justice, insure domestic Tranquility, provide for the common defence, promote the general Welfare, and secure the Blessings of Liberty to ourselves and our Posterity, do ordain and establish this Constitution for the United States of America". (The preamble is quoted in the grammar of the day, from the original version of the Constitution).

Consider these words penned by the Second Continental Congress, July 4, 1776:

"When in the course of human events, it becomes necessary for on People to dissolve the political bands which have connected them with another, and to assume among the powers of the earth, the separate and equal station to which the laws of nature and nature's God entitle them, a decent respect to the opinions of mankind requires that they should declare the cause which impel them to the separation.

We hold these truths to be self-evident that all men are created equal, that they are endowed by their Creator with certain inalienable rights, that among these are life, liberty and the pursuit of happiness-...." *(Second Continental Congress, by unanimous declaration, July 4, 1776)*

It is important that you and I have a clear understanding regarding the reasoning and purpose for the founding of this nation, and it's Constitution, before we can discuss the relationship of civil law to Biblical laws. Each, in his own way and time, must decide if the basis upon which our laws are established. You and you alone must study the evidence, even where you disagree, and arrive at a conclusion you can live by. This book is a compilation of individual thoughts and those published by others. Credit is given to those that authored articles and writings included in this text. It is hoped that this book will urge you to a greater understanding and spur you to research beyond these contents.

Thomas N. Culpepper
Author

INTRODUCTION

Having spent thirty seven years in law enforcement, I have observed how our laws affect citizens. I often made me wonder, just where did our system of laws and courts get their birth? Having spent some time in study of the law and its application, I thought it reasonable to lay out an explanation and some background on that very topic. It is my intent to help you develop a desire to know more about our judicial system and is origin and to inspire you to research the topic on your own. I trust that you will find this brief book informative and motivating. Remember, laws are for our good, those that obey them need not fear those that enforce them.

There have been voluminous discussions regarding the origins of our laws and the Constitution. Many believe that our Constitution and its subsequent Bill of Rights were based on strong religious belief, which is Christian belief. This book is a look into that topic and seeks to generate a desire of your own to search the facts so that you can stand firm on the knowledge that what you believe is indeed fact. First, we must look at the meaning of some of the words contained in the preamble of the Constitution:

<u>We the people</u> = meaning all those residing within the boundaries of the United States, in a legal status as the times dictated. Each individual person collectively as a nation.

<u>A more perfect union</u> = The framers of the Constitution realized that the Articles of Confederation that existed at the time were not a perfect form of government, although it was monumentally more acceptable than what had previously ruled them and so they endeavored to improve on the system so as to provide freedoms not granted under the King (an absolute monarchy). Even after crafting the constitution it was apparent that there were places where improvement must be made. The Constitution that resulted has been regarded as the finest establishing document for any government known then and now.

<u>Justice</u> = to have access to a judicial system for all people regardless of their station in life. A system that is not based on political position, economic status or ruling class affiliation. A system that is fair, equal and speedy. A system that provides for defense of accused persons and judgement by their peers ("we the people").

<u>Domestic tranquility</u> = to ensure that the domestic condition of society (society within the United States) is stable and not usurped by distrust, corruption, violent upheaval or unrest. That domestic differences are expressed in a manner that upholds the freedom of grievance and does not infringe on the rights of dissenting parties or those that may agree with the opposition.

<u>Common Defence</u> = To ensure that the borders of this nation were protected and controlled so as not to permit a detrimental number of aliens from flooding the

nation, without being able to provide for such. Also, to ensure that the interests of the nation abroad and its allies are defended.

<u>No</u> = No meant "NO" to the framers of our constitution. In the First Amendment they state that Congress shall make no law... Perhaps we have drifted away from the absolute intention of this word?

<u>All Men</u> = One might argue the use of this word at the time of the writing of the Constitution, however, I believe that the Framers of our Constitution fully intended that to mean all persons created by the living God, despite the common referral of the day to only the white, Anglo-Saxon, male population. As such, we today, should view that term to mean exactly that, all persons! In fact, I interpret it to mean persons unborn as well.

The United States of America, founded by men who were dedicated to the idea that mankind was born with certain "unalienable" or "natural rights". These were rights granted by the God that created the universe and were inviolable by any man, even a monarch. The idea of "natural rights" was contentious to the crown inasmuch as the King believed himself to be divinely appointed to rule. The events leading to the writing and, publishing of the Declaration of Independence, are testament to that fact.

"We hold these truths to be self-evident, that all men are created equal and are endowed by their Creator with certain unalienable rights, among these are life, liberty and the pursuit of happiness".

"The United States of America is a nation founded on the principle of law. For more than two hundred and forty years we have steadfastly remained loyal to our legal system. Our laws were, and are founded on a greater principle than mere man could conceive. Our legal system stems from centuries under the rule of others. Consider the following:

Feudal law was the order of the day in ancient England and other monarchies. Under the feudal system persons had only those rights to life, liberty and happiness that the Kind decided. In other words, the people existed solely for the benefit of the King." Lets look briefly at the structure of the feudal system:

King & Queen
(held all the power and ruled with their interest utmost)

Nobles
(Tended to land issues and reported to
the crown. Generally wealthy)

Knights
(Served in the crusades for the crown. Would be
pardoned by the Pope for past and present sins
committed as a benefit of service to the crown)

PEASANTS

(These were the working class masses. Generally
conducted farm labor or menial labor. Served
the crown with little or no benefit)

As indicated above, the smallest class was the ruling class. This class did not arrive at their level due to hard work, initiative, long hours and personal investment. The "feudal system", or "ruling class" existed because they people and families were given, bequeathed, or "coronated" into their position based on their birth, with the only expectation being, to sustain the line of the elite ruling class.

In examining the feudal system, one can easily discern that the colonists were very weary of their oppression, especially since it was imposed by an absent, oppressive and emotionally distant king. The feudal system did not put the interests of the masses at the forefront. Generally the crown held interest in what made the crown better off despite the treatment of the masses.

In his A Dissertation on the Canon and Feudal Law in 1765, John Adams wrote;

"Suppose a nation in some distant land should take the Bible for the only law book, and every member should regulate his conduct by the precepts there exhibited! Every member would be obliged in conscience, to temperance, frugality, and industry; to justice, kindness, and charity towards his fellow men; and to piety, love and reverence toward Almighty God…What a Utopia, what a Paradise would this region be."

One can sense the desire of Mr. Adams for a nation that would live by the purest of laws, but realized that that was an impossible task with human beings.

It is not difficult to see why the Founding Fathers committed such a treasonous and desperate act as declaring independence from King George. The Founding Fathers and those living in the colonies, for the most part, were keenly aware of the unholy and oppressive treatment they were receiving from a distant sovereign. As a nation that was established upon the principles of Christian love, charity and forbearance, the fledgling nation, known only as the "colonies", were moved to action. And action they did take, for on July 4th, 1776 men of various backgrounds and stations in life gathered in a small, hot, crowded hall and committed an act of treason; they signed the Declaration of Independence. This act could mean certain death to the signers, should they be apprehended and ultimately cost the lives of many seeking to be free.

The men and women of the colonies had to ask themselves the singular question, "at what cost liberty?'. As history reminds us, the fight for liberty was hard fought and was worth the fight. True freedom always has a high price, when measured against any nation on the planet, even with all her imperfections and scars from in-fighting, social and political conflict, the United States of America is far better off and offers more freedom than any other. The founders of the this nation held to the belief that bowing to the every demand of those that seek to persecute and destroy you only leads to a subservient life under the thumb of dictator. In our society today we have those that proclaim the virtues of other types of government, specifically socialism. Those that do not understand the final stage of socialism is communism, blindly accept the false belief that our system of government is inherently wrong. They believe in a "fairy tale" system that promises government that provides for your every need and all are stationed equally in life. Unfortunately that is not the reality of a world existence. The most glaring example currently is North Korea, where, as I have heard it said by others, "the only fat guy in North Korea is the Dictator, Kim Jung Un *(the dictator of North Korea at the time of this writing)*". We can trace the breakdown, of understanding that our Republic offers more freedom than anywhere else on the plant, to a failure to teach true American history and civics in our schools. When we alter the standard of what history is and fail to teach its core values, as our Founders believed, we veer off track and our society changes from an industrious, free nation to one that relies on the oppression of its people. I am not sure who said this first but is rings true today, "The government that provides everything for you can take everything from you" *(Author Unknown)*

In the declaration of Independence the framers understood what they were risking. They made their motivation clear when they penned, *"...That to secure these rights, governments are instituted among men, deriving their just powers from the consent of the governed, that whenever any form of government becomes destructive of these ends, it is the right of the people to alter or abolish it, and to institute new government, laying its foundation on such principles, and organizing its powers in such form, as to them shall seem most likely to affect their safety and happiness....." (Declaration of Independence 1776).*

*Article IV, Section 2 of the U.S. Constitution reminds us that, "The **citizens** of each State shall be entitled to all privileges and immunities of citizens in the several states".*

It is clear that those residing in the colonies, at this time were neither offered nor guaranteed any such privileges or immunities. The rights that were denied the colonies were those rights described in the Constitution as "Natural Rights", those rights bestowed only by God and unrightly denied to man by man. Let us take a look at the Founders of our Nation.

WHO WERE THE SIGNERS

"To have a clear grasp of where and why our laws were established, we must know the founders and what they committed themselves to. WE are all familiar with the with the names of John Adams, Alexander Hamilton, and Benjamin Franklin, but what of the others? Have you ever wondered what happened to the fifty-six men who signed the Declaration of Independence? This is the price they paid for the liberty we enjoy today:

Five signers were captured by the British as traitors, and tortured before they died. Twelve had their homes ransacked and burned. Two lost their sons in the revolutionary army, another had two sons captured. Nine of the fifty-six fought and died from wounds or hardships resulting from the Revolutionary War.

These men signed, and they pledged their lives, their fortunes, and their sacred honor! While putting ones honor in jeopardy today means little to many, in that day, honor was considered of supreme importance. Without honor, you had nothing to stand upon.

What kind of men were they? Twenty-four were lawyers and jurists. Eleven were merchants. Nine were farmers and large plantation owners. All were men of means, well educated (many were educated in seminaries). When they signed the Declaration of Independence they knew full well that the penalty for treason would be death if they were captured.

Carter Braxton of Virginia, a wealthy planter and trader, saw his ships swept from the seas by the British navy.

John Hart was dead from exhaustion and a broken heart 1n 1779.

Norris and Livingston suffered similar fates.

New Jersey's Richard Stockton was betrayed by a loyalist, imprisoned, beaten and nearly starved. His home burned and pillaged, he died in 1781 a broken man.

William Ellery of Rhode Island, also had his home burned.

After Lewis Morris of New York signed the Declaration, British troops ravaged his 2,000-acre estate and drove his family off the land.

Philip Livingston sold off everything and gave the money to the Revolution. He died in 1778.

Arthur Middleton, Edward Rutledge and Thomas Heyward Jr. went home to South Carolina. Heyward was wounded and all three were captured. As he rotted on a prison ship in St. Augustine. Other Southern signers suffered the same general fate.

Among the first to sign had been John Hancock, who wrote in big, bold script so George III "could read my name without spectacles and could now double his reward for 500 pounds for my head." If the cause of the revolution commands it, roared Hancock, "Burn Boston and make John Hancock a beggar!"

They all had a dream, a dream of a nation founded on the liberty of each individual with rights guaranteed to him or her by a source far greater then mortal man

"Our nation has drifted, and continues to do so, far away from intent of the Framers. As I read my copy of the constitution, I am emboldened by the realization that our fundamental principles are clearly influenced by the Holy Scriptures. Look at the foundational laws found in the Bible dealing with topics such as conduct among people, then examine the constitution and accompanying amendments. The Framers were not attentive to the thoughts coming out of the Enlightenment, although their legal mentors, like John Locke and Charles de Montesquieu, wrote their philosophies of the law from a Biblical world view. John Locke's book entitled *"The Reasonableness of Christianity"*, had such an influence on the thinking of most colonists in that day. Also, John Adams, a committed Christian, had just completed his book entitled *"A Defense of the Constitutions of Government of the United States"* and because of his stature as a statesman and his known Christian faith, it is supposed that his book may have been r read by the delegates to the convention. However, Adams did not attend this convention due to his service as Minister to England. *"Defense of the Constitutions of Government of the United States, John Adams, 1787."*

Returning to the idea of biblical laws, firstly, one set of rules was established by the God of the universe and are perfect in their design and purpose. The other was established by men of faulty character, albeit trying to do the best they could to interpreted God's call to action. We know the story of our Constitution and its signing on July 4th, 1776, but that is not the end of the story.

A short two years after ratification of the Constitution, a convention was called to add amendments to the newly created constitution, where the writers stated that they:

"*expressed a desire, in order to prevent misconstruction or abuse of its powers, that further declaratory and restrictive clauses should be added: and as extending the ground of public confidence in the government, will best ensure the beneficent ends of its institution…*". (in the Congress of the United States,1789).

THE CODE OF
HAMMURABI

Where did we first get the idea of needing codified laws? Let's take a look at <u>Hammurabi's Code</u>, created ca. 1780 B.C.E., is one of the earliest sets of laws found and one of the best preserved examples of this type of document from ancient Mesopotamia. The code is a collection of the legal decisions made by Hammurabi during his reign as king of Babylon, inscribed on a stele.

The text contains a list of crimes and their various punishments, as well as settlements for common disputes and guidelines for citizens' conduct. It focuses on theft, property damage, women's rights, marriage rights, children's rights, slave rights, murder, death, and injury. The Code does not specify a procedure for defense against charges, though it does imply one's right to present evidence. Similar to our right to subpoena witnesses and examine evidence. The stele was openly displayed for all to see; thus, no one could plead ignorance of the law as an excuse. This is also similar to our laws that are open for anyone to examine and study. Our system of justice has given over to legal counsel for such tasks, however we still retain the right to defend ourselves. Because it is assumed that very few could read during this time period, that much of the code was passed down through oral communication.

Although a social hierarchy placed some in privileged positions, the code proscribed punishments applicable to all classes, notwithstanding that punishments varied depending on the status of offenders and victims. Does this not sound familiar to our system of equal justice (although some would challenge that statement todays)?

As the rule of conduct was binding on all members of the community, state, and nation, the code provided coherent boundaries for citizens in a complex society. Citizens understood that abiding by these rules meant freedom to live and prosper. Although punishments for many minor infractions appear draconian by contemporary standards, the code formalized the fundamental responsibility of the individual to act in the context of the public interest. The code was grounded in commonly accepted principles of morality and ethics and provided a clear set of norms for all members of society to live together in peace.

HISTORICAL BACKGROUND

The Code of Hammurabi was one of many sets of laws in the Ancient Near East. Most of these law codes, coming from similar cultures and racial groups in a relatively small geographical area, necessarily have passages that resemble each other. For example, the laws found in the later Hittite code of laws (ca. 1300 B.C.E.) have some individual laws that bear a passing resemblance to those in the Code of Hammurabi, as well as other codices from the same geographic area. The earlier Ur-Nammu, of the written literature prolific Ur-III dynasty (twenty-first century B.C.E.), also produced a code of laws, some of which bear resemblance to certain specific laws in the Code of Hammurabi. The later Mosaic Law (according to the modern documentary hypothesis ca. 700–500 B.C.E. – under Hezekiah/Josiah; traditionally ca. 1200 B.C.E. – under Moses) also has some laws that resemble the Code of Hammurabi, as well as other law codes of the region." (https://www.newworldencyclopedia.org/Entry/CodeofHammurabi)

The 613 Laws of the Old Testament Called the Mitzvoth

One cannot possibly understand where our laws of today derive their origin unless we examine where the laws of the ancients originated. To clearly understand why we live in a nation of laws, we must look at our heritage and how and why laws were given to us.

The Hebrew word for "LAW" is *Torah*. In its most limited definition it refers to the Pentateuch. Yet, the word, Torah, is used to speak of the entire Old Testament as well.

The Law is the revealed mind of God. His Will is His commandment, and His commandment is His Law. Thus, the Law is Divine since it comes from a Divine source. It is also perfect, as God Himself is perfect. God's Law supersedes all other laws. It transcends all other law, making it the Supreme Law of the entire earth.

God's Law is also comprehensive and universal. It speaks to all areas of life, and to every living soul upon the face of the earth. The Law speaks of ceremonial truths, moral truths and dietary truths. It speaks of man's duty toward God, and man's duty toward his fellow man.

The Law addresses, philosophy, psychology, biology, physics, all other sciences, economics, ecology, Theology, culture, politics, military relations, international and domestic relations, family life, church life, business, criminal and civil law, and every other aspect of life thinkable. There is nothing that God's Law fails to address specifically. God regulates all life by His perfect Law. The New Testament is just as much God's Law as the Torah.

The following list will help in understanding the division of God's Old Testament Law, which the Hebrews have recorded, as numbering 613.

If we combine both Old and New Testament as One Law, the list grows and becomes more comprehensive. Yet, what we find in the New Testament is simply an augmentation of what is already contained in the Old Testament. The following expresses what the laws of the Old Testament were and how they were codified.

REGARDING RELATIONSHIP TO GOD

1. To know that God exists (Ex. 20:2; Deut. 5:6)
2. Not to entertain the idea that there is any god but the Eternal (Ex. 20:3)
3. Not to blaspheme (Ex. 22:27–28, Lev 24:16)
4. To hallow God's name (Lev. 22:32)
5. Not to profane God's name (Lev. 22:32)
6. To know that God is One, a complete Unity (Deut. 6:4)

7. To love God (Deut. 6:5)
8. To fear Him reverently (Deut. 6:13; 10:20)
9. Not to put the word of God to the test (Deut. 6:16)
10. .To imitate His good and upright ways (Deut. 28:9)

REGARDING RELATIONSHIP TO THE LAW

11. To honor the old and the wise (Lev. 19:32)
12. To learn Torah and to teach it (Deut. 6:7)
13. To cleave to those who know Him (Deut. 10:20)
14. Not to add to the commandments of the Torah. (Deut.13:1)
15. Not to take away from the commandments of the Torah (Deut.13:1)
16. That every person shall write a scroll of the Torah for himself (Deut. 31:19)

REGARDING SIGNS AND SYMBOLS
REGARDING THE COVENANT

17. To circumcise the male offspring (Gen. 17:12; Lev. 12:3)
18. To put fringes on the corners of clothing (Num. 15:38)
19. To bind God's Word on the head (Deut. 6:8)
20. To bind God's Word on the arm (Deut. 6:8)
21. To affix the mezuzah to the door posts and gates of your house (Deut. 6:9)

REGARDING LAWS ABOUT PRAYER AND BLESSING

22. To pray to God (Ex. 23:25; Deut. 6:13)
23. To read the *Shema* in the morning and at night (Deut. 6:7)
24. To recite grace after meals (Deut. 8:10)
25. Not to lay down a stone for worship (Lev. 26:1)

REGARDING LAWS ABOUT TO LOVE AND BROTHERHOOD

26. To love all human beings who are of the covenant (Lev. 19:18)
27. Not to stand by idly when a human life is in danger (Lev. 19:16)
28. Not to wrong any one in speech (Lev. 25:17)
29. Not to carry tales (Lev. 19:16)
30. Not to cherish hatred in one's heart (Lev. 19:17)
31. Not to take revenge (Lev. 19:18)
32. Not to bear a grudge (Lev. 19:18)
33. Not to put any Jew to shame (Lev. 19:17)
34. Not to curse any other Israelite (Lev. 19:14)
35. Not to give occasion to the simple-minded to stumble on the road (Lev. 19:14)
36. To rebuke the sinner (Lev. 19:17)
37. To relieve a neighbor of his burden and help to unload his beast (Ex. 23:5)
38. To assist in replacing the load upon a neighbor's beast (Deut.22:4)

39.   Not to leave a beast, that has fallen down beneath its burden, unaided (Deut. 22:4)

REGARDING LAWS ON TREATMENT OF THE POOR AND UNFORTUNATE

40.   Not to afflict an orphan or a widow (Ex. 22:21)

41.   Not to reap the entire field (Lev. 19:9; Lev. 23:22)

42.   To leave the unreaped corners of the field or orchard for the poor(Lev. 19:9)

43.   Not to gather gleanings (the ears that have fallen to the ground while reaping) (Lev. 19:9)

44.   To leave the gleanings for the poor (Lev. 19:9)

45.   Not to gather the imperfect clusters, of the vineyard (Lev. 19:10)

46.   To leave the imperfect clusters of the vineyard for the poor (Lev. 19:10; Deut. 24:21)

47.   Not to gather the single grapes that have fallen to the ground (Lev. 19:10)

48.   To leave the single grapes of the vineyard for the poor (Lev. 19:10)

49.   Not to return to take a forgotten sheaf (Deut. 24:19) This applies to all fruit trees (Deut. 24:20)

50.   To leave the forgotten sheaves for the poor (Deut. 24:19-20)

51.   Not to refrain from maintaining a poor man and giving him what he needs (Deut. 15:7)

52.   To give charity according to one's means (Deut. 15:11)

REGARDING LAWS ABOUT THE TREATMENT OF GENTILES

(the poor or strangers in today's parlance, {clarification added})

53.   To love the stranger (Deut. 10:19).
54.   Not to wrong the stranger in speech (Ex. 22:20)
55.   Not to wrong the stranger in buying or selling (Ex. 22:20)
56.   Not to intermarry with gentiles (Deut. 7:3)
57.   To exact the debt of an alien (Deut. 15:3)
58.   To lend to an alien at interest (Deut. 23:21)

REGARDING MARRIAGE, DIVORCE AND FAMILY

59.   To honor father and mother (Ex. 20:12)
60.   Not to smite a father or a mother (Ex. 21:15)
61.   Not to curse a father or mother (Ex. 21:17)
62.   To reverently fear father and mother (Lev. 19:3)
63.   To be fruitful and multiply (Gen. 1:28)
64.   That a eunuch shall not marry a daughter of Israel (Deut. 23:2)
65.   That a bastard shall not marry the daughter of a Jew (Deut.23:3)
66.   That an Ammonite or Moabite shall never marry the daughter of an Israelite (Deut. 23:4)
67.   Not to exclude a descendant of Esau from the community of Israel for three generations (Deut. 23:8-9)

68. Not to exclude an Egyptian from the community of Israel for three generations (Deut. 23:8-9)

69. That there shall be no harlot (in Israel); that is, that there shall be no intercourse with a woman, without previous marriage with a deed of marriage and formal declaration of marriage (Deut.23:18)

70. To take a wife by the sacrament of marriage (Deut.24:1)

71. That the newly married husband shall (be free) for one year to rejoice with his wife (Deut. 24:5)

72. That a bridegroom shall be exempt for a whole year from taking part in any public labor, such as military service, guarding the wall and similar duties (Deut. 24:5)

73. Not to withhold food, clothing or conjugal rights from a wife (Ex. 21:10)

74. That the woman suspected of adultery shall be dealt with as prescribed in the Torah (Num. 5:30)

75. That one who defames his wife's honor must live with her all his lifetime (Deut. 22:19)

76. That a man may not divorce his wife concerning whom he has published an evil report (Deut. 22:19)

77. To divorce by a formal written document (Deut. 24:1)

78. That one who divorced his wife shall not remarry her, if after the divorce she had been married to another man (Deut. 24:4)

79. That a widow whose husband died childless must not be married to anyone but her deceased husband's brother (Deut. 25:5)

80. To marry the widow of a brother who has died childless (Deut.25:5)

81. That the widow formally release the brother-in-law (if he refuses to marry her) (Deut. 25:7-9)

REGARDINGLAWS REGARDING FORBIDEEN SEXUAL RELATIONS

82. Not to indulge in familiarities with relatives, such as sensual kissing, carnal embracing, or provocative winking which may lead to incest (Lev.18:6)

83. Not to commit incest with one's mother (Lev. 18:7)

84. Not to commit sodomy with one's father (Lev. 18:7)

85. Not to commit incest with one's father's wife (Lev. 18:8)

86. Not to commit incest with one's sister (Lev. 18:9)

87. Not to commit incest with one's father's wife's daughter (Lev.18:9)

88. Not to commit incest with one's son's daughter (Lev. 18:10)

89. Not to commit incest with one's daughter's daughter (Lev.18:10)

90. Not to commit incest with one's daughter (this is not explicitly in the Torah but is inferred from other explicit commands that would include it)

91. Not to commit incest with one's fathers sister (Lev. 18:12)

92. Not to commit incest with one's mother's sister (Lev. 18:13)

93. Not to commit incest with one's father's brothers wife (Lev.18:14)

94. Not to commit sodomy with one's father's brother (Lev. 18:14)

95. Not to commit incest with one's son's wife (Lev. 18:15)

96. Not to commit incest with one's brother's wife (Lev. 18:16)

97. Not to commit incest with one's wife's daughter (Lev. 18:17)

98. Not to commit incest with the daughter of one's wife's son (Lev.18:17)

99. Not to commit incest with the daughter of one's wife's daughter (Lev. 18:17)

100. Not to commit incest with one's wife's sister (Lev. 18:18)

101. Not to have intercourse with a woman, in her menstrual period (Lev. 18:19)

102. Not to have intercourse with another man's wife (Lev. 18:20)

103. Not to commit sodomy with a male (Lev. 18:22)

104. Not to have intercourse with a beast (Lev. 18:23)

105. That a woman shall not have intercourse with a beast (Lev.18:23

106. Not to castrate the male of any species; neither a man, nor a domestic or wild beast, nor a fowl (Lev. 22:24)

REGARDING LAWS ABOUT THE TIMES AND SEASONS

107. That the new month shall be solemnly proclaimed as holy, and the months and years shall be calculated by the Supreme Court only (Ex. 12:2)

108. Not to travel on the Sabbath outside the limits of one's place of residence (Ex. 16:29)

109. To sanctify the Sabbath (Ex. 20:8)

110. Not to do work on Sabbath (Ex. 20:10)

111. To rest on Sabbath (Ex. 23:12; 34:21)

112. To celebrate the festivals (Ex.23:14)

113. To rejoice on the festivals (Deut. 16:14)

114. To appear in the Sanctuary on the festivals (Deut. 16:16)

115. To remove leaven on the Eve of Passover (Ex. 12:15)

116. To rest on the first day of Passover (Ex. 12:16; Lev. 23:7)

117. Not to do work on the first day of Passover (Ex. 12:16; Lev.23:6-7)

118. To rest on the seventh day of Passover (Ex. 12:16; Lev. 23:8)

119. Not to do work on the seventh day of Passover (Ex. 12:16;Lev. 23:8)

120. To eat "matzah" [unleavened bread] on the first night of Passover (Ex. 12:18)

121. That no leaven be in the Israelite's possession during Passover (Ex. 12:19)

122. Not to eat any food containing leaven on Passover (Ex.12:20)

123. Not to eat leaven on Passover (Ex. 13:3)

124. That leaven shall not be seen in an Israelite's home during Passover (Ex. 13:7)

125. To discuss the departure from Egypt on the first night of Passover (Ex. 13:8)

126. Not to eat leaven after mid-day on the fourteenth of Nissan (Deut. 16:3)

127. To count forty-nine days from the time of the cutting of the Omer (Lev. 23:15)

128. To rest on Pentecost (Lev. 23:21)

129. Not to do work on the feast of Pentecost (Lev. 23:21)

130. To rest on Rosh Hashanah (Lev. 23:24)

131. Not to do work on Rosh Hashanah (Lev. 23:25)

132. To hear the sound of the Trumpet (Num.29:1)

133. To fast on Yom Kippur (Lev. 23:27)

134. Not to eat or drink on Yom Kippur (Lev. 23:29)

135. Not to do work on Yom Kippur (Lev. 23:31)

136. To rest on the Yom Kippur (Lev. 23:32)

137. To rest on the first day of the feast of Tabernacles or Booths(Lev. 23:35)

138. Not to do work on the first day of the feast of Tabernacles. (Lev. 23:35)

139. To rest on the eighth day of the feast of Tabernacles (Lev.23:36)

140. Not to do work on the eighth day of the feast of Tabernacles (Lev. 23:36)

141. To take during Sukkot a palm branch and the other three plants (Lev. 23:40)

142. To dwell in booths seven days during Sukkot (Lev. 23:42)

REGARDING LAWS ABOUT
DIETARY PRACTICES

143. To examine the marks in cattle(Lev. 11:2)
144. Not to eat the flesh of unclean beasts (Lev. 11:4)
145. To examine the marks in fishes (so as to distinguish the clean from the unclean (Lev. 11:9)
146. Not to eat unclean fish (Lev. 11:11)
147. To examine the marks in fowl, so as to distinguish the clean from the unclean (Deut. 14:11)
148. Not to eat unclean fowl (Lev. 11:13)
149. To examine the marks in locusts, so as to distinguish the clean from the unclean (Lev. 11:21)
150. Not to eat a worm found in fruit (Lev. 11:41)
151. Not to eat of things that creep upon the earth (Lev. 11:41-42)
152. Not to eat any vermin of the earth (Lev. 11:44)
153. Not to eat things that swarm in the water (Lev. 11:43 and 46)
154. Not to eat of winged insects (Deut. 14:19)
155. Not to eat the flesh of a beast that is torn (Ex.22:30)
156. Not to eat the flesh of a beast that died of itself (Deut. 14:21)
157. To slay cattle, deer and fowl according to the law if their flesh is to be eaten (Deut. 12:21)
158. Not to eat a limb removed from a living beast (Deut. 12:23)
159. Not to slaughter an animal and its young on the same day (Lev.22:28)
160. Not to take the mother-bird with the young (Deut. 22:6)

161. To set the mother-bird free when taking the nest (Deut.22:6-7)
162. Not to eat the flesh of an ox that was condemned to be stoned (Ex. 21:28)
163. Not to boil meat with milk (Ex. 23:19)
164. Not to eat flesh with milk (Ex. 34:26)
165. Not to eat the of the thigh-vein which shrank (Gen. 32:33)
166. Not to eat the fat of the offering (Lev. 7:23)
167. Not to eat blood (Lev. 7:26)
168. To cover the blood of undomesticated animals and of fowl that have been killed (Lev. 17:13)
169. Not to eat or drink like a glutton or a drunkard (Lev. 19:26; Deut. 21:20)

REGARDING LAWS ABOUT BUSINESS PRACTICES

170. Not to do wrong in buying or selling (Lev. 25:14)
171. Not to make a loan to an Israelite on interest (Lev. 25:37)
172. Not to borrow on interest (Deut. 23:20)
173. Not to take part in any usurious transaction between borrower and lender, neither as a surety, nor as a witness, nor as a writer of the bond for them (Ex. 22:24)
174. To lend to a poor person (Ex. 22:24)
175. Not to demand from a poor man repayment of his debt, when the creditor knows that he cannot pay, nor press him (Ex.22:24)

176. Not to take in pledge utensils used in preparing food (Deut.24:6)
177. Not to exact a pledge from a debtor by force (Deut. 24:10)
178. Not to keep the pledge from its owner at the time when he needs it (Deut. 24:12)
179. To return a pledge to its owner (Deut. 24:13)
180. Not to take a pledge from a widow (Deut. 24:17)
181. Not to commit fraud in measuring (Lev. 19:35)
182. To ensure that scales and weights are correct (Lev. 19:36)
183. Not to possess inaccurate measures and weights (Deut.25:13-14)

REGARDING LAWS GOVERNING EMPLOYEES, SERVANTS AND SLAVES

184. Not to delay payment of a hired man's wages (Lev. 19:13)
185. That the hired laborer shall be permitted to eat of the produce he is reaping (Deut. 23:25-26)
186. That the hired laborer shall not take more than he can eat (Deut. 23:25)
187. That a hired laborer shall not eat produce that is not being harvested (Deut. 23:26)
188. To pay wages to the hired man at the due time (Deut. 24:15)
189. To deal judicially with the Hebrew bondman in accordance with the laws appertaining to him (Ex. 21:2-6)

190. Not to compel the Hebrew servant to do the work of a slave (Lev. 25:39)
191. Not to sell a Hebrew servant as a slave (Lev. 25:42)
192. Not to treat a Hebrew servant rigorously (Lev. 25:43)
193. Not to permit a gentile to treat harshly a Hebrew bondman sold to him (Lev. 25:53)
194. Not to send away a Hebrew bondman servant empty handed, when he is freed from service (Deut. 15:13)
195. To bestow liberal gifts upon the Hebrew bondsman (at the end of his term of service), and the same should be done to a Hebrew bondwoman (Deut. 15:14)
196. To redeem a Hebrew maid-servant (Ex. 21:8)
197. Not to sell a Hebrew maid-servant to another person (Ex. 21:8)
198. To espouse a Hebrew maid-servant (Ex. 21:8-9)
199. To keep the Canaanite slave forever (Lev. 25:46)
200. Not to surrender a slave, who has fled to the land of Israel, to his owner who lives outside Palestine (Deut. 23:16)
201. Not to wrong such a slave (Deut. 23:17)
202. Not to muzzle a beast, while it is working in produce which it can eat and enjoy (Deut. 25:4)

REGARDING LAWS ABOUT VOWS, OATHS AND SWEARING

203. That a man should fulfill whatever he has uttered (Deut. 23:24)

204. Not to swear needlessly (Ex. 20:7)
205. Not to violate an oath or swear falsely (Lev. 19:12)
206. To decide in cases of annulment of vows, according to the rules set forth in the Torah (Num. 30:2-17)
207. Not to break a vow (Num. 30:3)
208. To swear by His name truly (Deut. 10:20)
209. Not to delay in fulfilling vows or bringing vowed or free-will offerings (Deut. 23:22)

REGARDING LAWS COVERING THE SABATTACIAL AND JUBILEE YEARS

210. To let the land lie fallow in the Sabbatical year (Ex. 23:11; Lev.25:2)
211. To cease from tilling the land in the Sabbatical year (Ex. 23:11) (Lev. 25:2)
212. Not to till the ground in the Sabbatical year (Lev. 25:4)
213. Not to do any work on the trees in the Sabbatical year (Lev.25:4)
214. Not to reap the aftermath that grows in the Sabbatical year, in the same way as it is reaped in other years (Lev. 25:5)
215. Not to gather the fruit of the tree in the Sabbatical year in the same way as it is gathered in other years (Lev. 25:5)
216. To sound the Ram's horn in the Sabbatical year (Lev. 25:9)
217. To release debts in the seventh year (Deut. 15:2)

218. Not to demand return of a loan after the Sabbatical year has passed (Deut. 15:2)
219. Not to refrain from making a loan to a poor man, because of the release of loans in the Sabbatical year (Deut. 15:9)
220. To assemble the people to hear the Torah at the close of the seventh year (Deut. 31:12)
221. To count the years of the Jubilee by years and by cycles of seven years (Lev. 25:8)
222. To keep the Jubilee year holy by resting and letting the land lie fallow (Lev. 25:10)
223. Not to cultivate the soil nor do any work on the trees, in the Jubilee Year (Lev. 25:11)
224. Not to reap the aftermath of the field that grew of itself in the Jubilee Year, in the same way as in other years (Lev. 25:11)
225. Not to gather the fruit of the tree in the Jubilee Year, in the same way as in other years (Lev. 25:11)
226. To grant redemption to the land in the Jubilee year (Lev. 25:24)

REGARDING THE COURTS AND JUDICIAL PROCEDURE

227. To appoint judges and officers in every community of Israel (Deut. 16:18)
228. Not to appoint as a judge, a person who is not well versed in the laws of the Torah, even if he is expert in other branches of knowledge (Deut. 1:17)
229. To adjudicate cases of purchase and sale (Lev. 25:14)

230. To judge cases of liability of a paid depositary (Ex. 22:9)

231. To adjudicate cases of loss for which a gratuitous borrower is liable (Ex. 22:13-14)

232. To adjudicate cases of inheritances (Num. 27:8-11)

233. To judge cases of damage caused by an uncovered pit (Ex.21:33-34)

234. To judge cases of injuries caused by beasts (Ex. 21:35-36)

235. To adjudicate cases of damage caused by trespass of cattle (Ex.22:4)

236. To adjudicate cases of damage caused by fire (Ex. 22:5)

237. To adjudicate cases of damage caused by a gratuitous depositary (Ex. 22:6-7)

238. To adjudicate other cases between a plaintiff and a defendant (Ex. 22:8)

239. Not to curse a judge (Ex. 22:27)

240. That one who possesses evidence shall testify in Court (Lev.5:1)

241. Not to testify falsely (Ex. 20:13)

242. That a witness, who has testified in a capital case, shall not lay down the law in that particular case (Num. 35:30)

243. That a transgressor shall not testify (Ex. 23:1)

244. That the court shall not accept the testimony of a close relative of the defendant in matters of capital punishment (Deut. 24:16)

245. Not to hear one of the parties to a suit in the absence of the other party (Ex. 23:1)

246. To examine witnesses thoroughly (Deut. 13:15)

247. Not to decide a case on the evidence of a single witness (Deut.19:15)

248. To give the decision according to the majority, when there is a difference of opinion among the members of the Sanhedrin as to matters of law (Ex. 23:2)

249. Not to decide, in capital cases, according to the view of the majority, when those who are for condemnation exceed by one only, those who are for acquittal (Ex. 23:2)

250. That, in capital cases, one who had argued for acquittal, shall not later on argue for condemnation (Ex. 23:2)

251. To treat parties in a litigation with equal impartiality (Lev. 19:15)

252. Not to render iniquitous decisions (Lev. 19:15)

253. Not to favor a great man when trying a case (Lev. 19:15)

254. Not to take a bribe (Ex. 23:8)

255. Not to be afraid of a bad man, when trying a case (Deut. 1:17)

256. Not to be moved in trying a case, by the poverty of one of the parties (Ex. 23:3; Lev. 19:15)

257. Not to pervert the judgment of strangers or orphans (Deut.24:17)

258. Not to pervert the judgment of a sinner (a person poor in fulfillment of commandments) (Ex. 23:6)

259. Not to render a decision on one's personal opinion, but only on the evidence of two witnesses, who saw what actually occurred (Ex. 23:7)

260. Not to execute one guilty of a capital offense, before he has stood his trial (Num. 35:12)
261. To accept the rulings of every Supreme Court in Israel (Deut.17:11)
262. Not to rebel against the orders of the Court (Deut. 17:11)

REGARDING LAWS COVERING INJURIES AND DAMAGES (CIVIL LAWS)

263. To make a parapet for your roof (Deut. 22:8)
264. Not to leave something that might cause hurt (Deut. 22:8)
265. To save the pursued even at the cost of the life of the pursuer (Deut. 25:12)
266. Not to spare a pursuer, but he is to be slain before he reaches the pursued and slays the latter, or uncovers his nakedness (Deut. 25:12)

REGARDING LAWS ON PROPERTY AND PROPERTY RIGHTS

267. Not to sell a field in the land of Israel in perpetuity (Lev. 25:23)
268. Not to change the character of the open land (about the cities of) the Levites or of their fields; not to sell it in perpetuity, but it may be redeemed at any time (Lev. 25:34)

269. That houses sold within a walled city may be redeemed within a year (Lev. 25:29)
270. Not to remove landmarks (Deut. 19:14)
271. Not to swear falsely in denial of another's property rights (Lev.19:11)
272. Not to deny falsely another's property rights (Lev. 19:11)
273. Never to settle in the land of Egypt (Deut. 17:16)
274. Not to steal personal property (Lev. 19:11)
275. To restore that which one took by robbery (Lev. 5:23)
276. To return lost property (Deut. 22:1)
277. Not to pretend not to have seen lost property, to avoid the obligation to return it (Deut. 22:3)

REGARDING LAWS CONCERNING CRIMINAL ACTIONS

278. Not to slay an innocent person (Ex. 20:13)
279. Not to kidnap any person of Israel (Ex. 20:13)
280. Not to rob by violence (Lev. 19:13)
281. Not to defraud (Lev. 19:13)
282. Not to covet what belongs to another (Ex. 20:14)
283. Not to crave something that belongs to another (Deut. 5:18)
284. Not to indulge in evil thoughts and sights (Num. 15:39)

REGARDING LAWS DIRECTING PUNISHMENT AND RESTITUTION

285. That the Court shall pass sentence of death by decapitation with the sword (Ex. 21:20; Lev. 26:25)
286. That the Court shall pass sentence of death by strangulation (Lev. 20:10)
287. That the Court shall pass sentence of death by burning with fire (Lev. 20:14)
288. That the Court shall pass sentence of death by stoning (Deut.22:24)
289. To hang the dead body of one who has incurred that penalty (Deut. 21:22)
290. That the dead body of an executed criminal shall not remain hanging on the tree overnight (Deut. 21:23)
291. To inter the executed on the day of execution (Deut. 21:23)
292. Not to accept ransom from a murderer (Num. 35:31)
293. To exile one who committed accidental homicide (Num. 35:25)
294. To establish six cities of refuge (accidental homicide) (Deut. 19:3)
295. Not to accept ransom from an accidental homicide, so as to relieve him from exile (Num. 35:32)
296. To decapitate the heifer in the manner prescribed (in expiation of a murder on the road, the perpetrator of which remained undiscovered) (Deut. 21:4)
297. Not to plow nor sow the rough valley (Deut. 21:4)
298. To adjudge a thief to pay compensation or suffer death (Ex. 21:16; Ex. 21:37; Ex. 22:1)

299. That he who inflicts a bodily injury shall pay monetary compensation (Ex. 21:18-19)

300. To impose a penalty of fifty shekels upon the seducer and enforce the other rules in connection with the case (Ex. 22:15-16)

301. That the violator shall marry her (Deut. 22:28-29)

302. That one who has raped a damsel and has then married her, may not divorce her (Deut. 22:29)

303. Not to inflict punishment on the Sabbath (Ex. 35:3)

304. To punish the wicked by the infliction of stripes (Deut. 25:2)

305. Not to exceed the statutory number of stripes laid on one who has incurred that punishment (Deut. 25:3)

306. Not to spare the offender, in imposing the prescribed penalties on one who has caused damage (Deut. 19:13)

307. To do unto false witnesses as they had purposed to do (Deut. 19:19)

308. Not to punish anyone who has committed an offense under duress (Deut. 22:26)

REGARDING LAWS ABOUT PROPHECY

309. To heed the call of every prophet in each generation, provided that he neither adds to, nor takes away from the Torah (Deut.18:15)

310. Not to prophesy falsely (Deut. 18:20)

311. Not to refrain from putting a false prophet to death nor to be in fear of him (Deut. 18:22) (negative)

REGARDING LAWS ON IDOLATRY,
IDOLATERS AND IDOLATROUS PRACTICES

312. Not to make a graven image; neither to make it oneself nor to have it made by others (Ex. 20:4)
313. Not to make any figures for ornament, even if they are not worshipped (Ex. 20:20)
314. Not to make idols even for others (Ex. 34:17; Lev. 19:4)
315. Not to use the ornament of any object of idolatrous worship (Deut. 7:25)
316. Not to make use of an idol or its accessory objects, offerings, or libations (Deut. 7:26)
317. Not to drink wine of idolaters (Deut. 32:38)
318. Not to worship an idol in the way in which it is usually worshipped (Ex. 20:5)
319. Not to bow down to an idol, even if that is not its mode of worship (Ex. 20:5)
320. Not to prophesy in the name of an idol (Ex. 23:13; Deut.18:20)
321. Not to hearken to one who prophesies in the name of an idol (Deut. 13:4)
322. Not to lead the children of Israel astray to idolatry (Ex. 23:13)
323. Not to entice an Israelite to idolatry (Deut. 13:12)
324. 324.To destroy idolatry and its appurtenances (Deut. 12:2-3)
325. Not to love the enticer to idolatry (Deut. 13:9)
326. Not to give up hating the enticer to idolatry (Deut. 13:9)

327. Not to save the enticer from capital punishment, but to stand by at his execution (Deut. 13:9)

328. A person whom he attempted to entice to idolatry shall not urge pleas for the acquittal of the enticer (Deut. 13:9)

329. A person whom he attempted to entice shall not refrain from giving evidence of the enticer's guilt, if he has such evidence (Deut. 13:9)

330. Not to swear by an idol to its worshipers, nor cause them to swear by it (Ex. 23:13)

331. Not to turn one's attention to idolatry (Lev. 19:4)

332. Not to adopt the institutions of idolaters nor their customs (Lev. 18:3; Lev. 20:23)

333. Not to pass a child through the fire to Molech (Lev. 18:21)

334. Not to suffer any one practicing witchcraft to live (Ex. 22:17)

335. Not to practice observing times or seasons –i.e. astrology (Lev. 19:26)

336. Not to practice superstitions/witchcraft (doing things based on signs and potions; using charms and incantations, some may even interpret to mean astrology) (Lev. 19:26)

337. Not to consult familiar spirits or ghosts (Lev. 19:31)

338. Not to consult wizards (Lev. 19:31)

339. Not to practice specific magic by using stones herbs or objects. (Deut. 18:10)

340. Not to practice magical practices in general.(Deut. 18:10)

341. Not to practice the art of casting spells over snakes and scorpions (Deut. 18:11)

342. Not to enquire of a familiar spirit or ghost (Deut. 18:11)
343. Not to seek the dead (Deut. 18:11)
344. Not to enquire of a wizard) (Deut. 18:11)
345. Not to remove the entire beard, like the idolaters (Lev. 19:27)
346. Not to round the corners of the head, as the idolatrous priests do (Lev. 19:27)
347. Not to cut oneself or make incisions in one's flesh in grief, like the idolaters (Lev. 19:28; Deut. 14:1)
348. Not to tattoo the body like the idolaters (Lev. 19:28)
349. Not to make a bald spot for the dead (Deut. 14:1)
350. Not to plant a tree for worship (Deut. 16:21)
351. Not to set up a pillar (for worship) (Deut. 16:22)
352. Not to show favor to idolaters (Deut. 7:2)
353. Not to make a covenant with the seven nations (Ex. 23:32; Deut. 7:2)
354. Not to settle idolaters in our land (Ex. 23:33)
355. To slay the inhabitants of a city that has become idolatrous and burn that city (Deut. 13:16-17)
356. Not to rebuild a city that has been led astray to idolatry (Deut.13:17)
357. Not to make use of the property of city that has been so led astray (Deut. 13:18)

REGARDING LAWS ON AGRICULTURAL AND AMINIMAL HUSBANDRY

358. Not to cross-breed cattle of different species (Lev. 19:19)

359. Not to sow different kinds of seed together in one field (Lev.19:19)
360. Not to eat the fruit of a tree for three years from the time it was planted (Lev. 19:23)
361. That the fruit of fruit-bearing trees in the fourth year of their planting shall be sacred like the second tithe and eaten in Jerusalem (Lev. 19:24)
362. Not to sow grain or herbs in a vineyard (Deut. 22:9)
363. Not to eat the produce of diverse seeds sown in a vineyard (Deut. 22:9)
364. Not to work with beasts of different species, yoked together (Deut. 22:10)

REGARDING LAWS ABOUT CLOTHING

365. That a man shall not wear women's clothing (Deut. 22:5)
366. That a woman should not wear men's clothing (Deut. 22:5)
367. Not to wear garments made of wool and linen mixed together (Deut. 22:11)

REGARDING LAWS ABOUT THE FIRSTBORN

368. To redeem the firstborn human male (Ex. 13:13; Ex. 34:20; Num. 18:15)
369. To redeem the firstling of an ass (Ex. 13:13; Ex. 34:20)
370. To break the neck of the firstling of an ass if it is not redeemed (Ex. 13:13; Ex. 34:20)

371. Not to redeem the firstling of a clean beast (Num. 18:17)

REGARDING LAWS ABOUT THE HIGH PRIESTS, PRIETS AND LEVITES

372. That the Priest shall put on priestly vestments for the service (Ex. 28:2)
373. Not to tear the High Priest's robe (Ex. 28:32)
374. That the Priest shall not enter the Sanctuary at all times (i.e., at times when he is not performing service) (Lev. 16:2)
375. That the ordinary Priest shall not defile himself by contact with any dead, other than immediate relatives (Lev. 21:1-3)
376. That the sons of Aaron defile themselves for their deceased relatives, and mourn for them like other Israelites, who are commanded to mourn for their relatives (Lev.21:3)
377. That a Priest who had an immersion during the day (to cleanse him from his uncleanness) shall not serve in the Sanctuary until after sunset (Lev. 21:6)
378. That a Priest shall not marry a divorced woman (Lev. 21:7)
379. That a Priest shall not marry a harlot (Lev. 21:7)
380. That a Priest shall not marry a profaned woman (Lev. 21:7)
381. To show honor to a Priest, and to give him precedence in all things that are holy (Lev. 21:8)

382. That a High Priest shall not defile himself with any dead, even if they are relatives (Lev. 21:11)

383. That a High Priest shall not go (under the same roof) with a dead body (Lev. 21:11)

384. That the High Priest shall marry a virgin (Lev. 21:13)

385. That the High Priest shall not marry a widow (Lev. 21:14)

386. That the High Priest shall not cohabit with a widow, even without marriage, because he profanes her (Lev. 21:15)

387. That a person with a physical blemish shall not serve (in the Sanctuary) (Lev. 21:17)

388. That a Priest with a temporary blemish shall not serve there (Lev. 21:21)

389. That a person with a physical blemish shall not enter the Sanctuary further than the altar (Lev. 21:23)

390. That a Priest who is unclean shall not serve (in the Sanctuary) (Lev. 22:2-3)

391. To send the unclean out of the Camp, that is, out of the Sanctuary (Num. 5:2)

392. That a Priest who is unclean shall not enter the courtyard (Num. 5:2-3)

393. That the sons or descendants of Aaron shall bless Israel (Num. 6:23)

394. To set apart a portion of the dough for the Priest (Num.15:20)

395. That the Levites shall not occupy themselves with the service that belongs to the sons of Aaron, nor the sons of Aaron with that belonging to the Levites (Num. 18:3)

396. That one not a descendant of Aaron in the male line shall not serve (in the Sanctuary) (Num. 18:4-7)
397. That the Levite shall serve in the Sanctuary (Num. 18:23)
398. To give the Levites cities to dwell in, these to serve also as cities of refuge (Num. 35:2)
399. That none of the tribe of Levi shall take any portion of territory in the land (of Israel) (Deut. 18:1)
400. That none of the tribe of Levi shall take any share of the spoil (Deut. 18:1)
401. That the sons of Aaron shall serve in the Sanctuary in divisions, but on festivals, they all serve together (Deut. 18:6-8)

REGARDING LAWS ABOUT TITHES, TAXES AND T'RUMAH

402. That an uncircumcised person shall not shall not eat of the t'rumah, and the same applies to other holy things. This rule is inferred from the law of the Paschal offering, by similarity of phrase (Ex. 12:44-45 and Lev. 22:10)
403. Not to alter the order of separating the t'rumah and the tithes; the separation be in the order first-fruits at the beginning, then the t'rumah, then the first tithe, and last the second tithe (Ex.22:28)
404. To give half a shekel every year (to the Sanctuary for provision of the public sacrifices) (Ex. 30:13)
405. That a priest who is unclean shall not eat of the t'rumah (Lev.22:3-4)

406. That a person who is not a kohein or the wife or unmarried daughter of a kohein shall not eat of the t'rumah (Lev. 22:10)

407. That a sojourner with a kohein or his hired servant shall not eat of the t'rumah (Lev. 22:10)

408. Not to eat unholy things (Lev. 22:15)

409. To set apart the tithe of the produce for the Levites (Lev. 27:30; Num.18:24)

410. To tithe cattle (Lev. 27:32)

411. Not to sell the tithe of the heard (Lev. 27:32–33)

412. That the Levites shall set apart a tenth of the tithes, which they had received from the Israelites, and give it to the Priest (Num. 18:26)

413. Not to eat the second tithe of cereals outside Jerusalem (Deut.12:17)

414. Not to consume the second tithe of the vintage outside of Jerusalem (Deut. 12:17)

415. Not to consume the second tithe of the oil outside of Jerusalem (Deut. 12:17)

416. Not to forsake the Levites (Deut. 12:19); but their gifts should be given to them, so that they might rejoice therewith on each and every festival

417. To set apart the second tithe in the first, second, fourth and fifth years of the sabbatical cycle to be eaten by its owner in Jerusalem (Deut. 14:22)

418. To set apart the second tithe in the third and sixth year of the sabbatical cycle for the poor (Deut. 14:28–29)

419. To give the kohein the due portions of the carcass of cattle (Deut. 18:3)

420. To give the first of the fleece to the priest (Deut. 18:4)
421. To set apart a small portion of the grain, wine and oil for the Priest (Deut.18:4)
422. Not to expend the proceeds of the second tithe on anything but food and drink (Deut. 26:14)
423. Not to eat the Second Tithe, even in Jerusalem, in a state of uncleanness, until the tithe had been redeemed (Deut. 26:14)
424. Not to eat the Second Tithe, when mourning (Deut. 26:14)
425. To make the declaration, when bringing the second tithe to the Sanctuary (Deut. 26:13)

REGARDING LAWS ABOUT THE TEMPLE, THE SANCTUARY AND SCARED OBJECTS

426. Not to build an altar of hewn stone (Ex. 20:22)
427. Not to mount the altar by steps (Ex. 20:23)
428. To build the Sanctuary (Ex. 25:8)
429. Not to remove the staves from the Ark (Ex. 25:15)
430. To set the showbread and the frankincense before the Lord every Sabbath (Ex. 25:30)
431. To kindle lights in the Sanctuary (Ex. 27:21)
432. That the breastplate shall not be loosened from the ephod (Ex.28:28)
433. To offer up incense twice daily (Ex. 30:7)
434. Not to offer strange incense nor any sacrifice upon the golden altar (Ex. 30:9)

435. That the Priest shall wash his hands and feet at the time of service (Ex. 30:19)

436. To prepare the oil of anointment and anoint high priests and kings with it (Ex. 30:31)

437. Not to compound oil for lay use after the formula of the anointing oil (Ex. 30:32-33)

438. Not to anoint a stranger with the anointing oil (Ex. 30:32)

439. Not to compound anything after the formula of the incense (Ex.30:37)

440. That he who, in error, makes unlawful use of sacred things, shall make restitution of the value of his trespass and add a fifth (Lev. 5:16)

441. To remove the ashes from the altar (Lev. 6:3)

442. To keep fire always burning on the altar of the burnt-offering (Lev. 6:6)

443. Not to extinguish the fire on the altar (Lev. 6:6)

444. That a kohein shall not enter the Sanctuary with disheveled hair (Lev. 10:6)

445. That a kohein shall not enter the Sanctuary with torn garments (Lev. 10:6)

446. That the kohein shall not leave the Courtyard of the Sanctuary, during service (Lev. 10:7)

447. That an intoxicated person shall not enter the Sanctuary nor give decisions in matters of the Law (Lev. 10:9-11)

448. To revere the Sanctuary (Lev. 19:30)

449. That when the Ark is carried, it should be carried on the shoulder (Num. 7:9)

450. To observe the second Passover (Num. 9:11)

451. To eat the flesh of the Paschal lamb on it, with unleavened bread and bitter herbs (Num. 9:11)

452. Not to leave any flesh of the Paschal lamb brought on the second Passover until the morning (Num. 9:12)

453. Not to break a bone of the Paschal lamb brought on the second Passover (Num. 9:12)

454. To sound the trumpets at the offering of sacrifices and in times of trouble (Num. 10:9-10)

455. To watch over the edifice continually (Num. 18:2)

456. Not to allow the Sanctuary to remain unwatched (Num. 18:5)

457. That an offering shall be brought by one who has in error committed a trespass against sacred things, or robbed, or lain carnally with a bond-maid betrothed to a man, or denied what was deposited with him and swore falsely to support his denial. This is called a guilt-offering for a known trespass (Lev. 5:15-19)

458. Not to destroy anything of the Sanctuary, of synagogues, or of houses of study, nor erase the holy names (of God); nor may sacred scriptures be destroyed (Deut. 12:2-4)

REGARDING LAWS ABOUT SCARIFICES AND OFFERINGS

459. To sanctify the firstling of clean cattle and offer it up (Ex. 13:2;Deut. 15:19)

460. To slay the Paschal lamb (Ex. 12:6)

461. To eat the flesh of the Paschal sacrifice on the night of the fifteenth of Nissan (Ex. 12:8)

462. Not to eat the flesh of the Paschal lamb raw or sodden (Ex.12:9)

463. Not to leave any portion of the flesh of the Paschal sacrifice until the morning unconsumed (Ex. 12:10)

464. Not to give the flesh of the Paschal lamb to an Israelite who had become an apostate (Ex. 12:43)

465. Not to give flesh of the Paschal lamb to a stranger who lives among you to eat (Ex. 12:45)

466. Not to take any of the flesh of the Paschal lamb from the company's place of assembly (Ex. 12:46)

467. Not to break a bone of the Paschal lamb (Ex. 12:46)

468. That the uncircumcised shall not eat of the flesh of the Paschal lamb (Ex. 12:48)

469. Not to slaughter the Paschal lamb while there is leaven in the home (Ex. 23:18; Ex. 24:25)

470. Not to leave the part of the Paschal lamb that should be burnt on the altar until the morning, when it will no longer be fit to be burnt (Ex. 23:18; Ex. 24:25)

471. Not to go up to the Sanctuary for the festival without bringing an offering (Ex. 23:15)

472. To bring the first fruits to the Sanctuary (Ex. 23:19)

473. That the flesh of a sin–offering and guilt–offering shall be eaten (Ex. 29:33)

474. That one not of the seed of Aaron, shall not eat the flesh of the holy sacrifices (Ex. 29:33)

475. To observe the procedure of the burnt–offering (Lev. 1:3)

476. To observe the procedure of the meal-offering (Lev. 2:1)
477. Not to offer up leaven or honey (Lev. 2:11)
478. That every sacrifice be salted (Lev. 2:13)
479. Not to offer up any offering unsalted (Lev. 2:13)
480. That the Court of Judgment shall offer up a sacrifice if they have erred in a judicial pronouncement (Lev. 4:13)
481. That an individual shall bring a sin-offering if he has sinned in error by committing a transgression (Lev. 4:27-28)
482. To offer a sacrifice of varying value in accordance with one's means (Lev. 5:7)
483. Not to sever completely the head of a fowl brought as a sin-offering (Lev. 5:8)
484. Not to put olive oil in a sin-offering made of flour (Lev. 5:11)
485. Not to put frankincense on a sin-offering made of flour (Lev.5:11)
486. That an individual shall bring an offering if he is in doubt as to whether he has committed a sin for which one has to bring a sin-offering. (Lev.5:17-19)
487. That the remainder of the meal offerings shall be eaten (Lev.6:9)
488. Not to allow the remainder of the meal offerings to become leavened (Lev. 6:10)
489. That the High Priest shall offer a meal offering daily (Lev. 6:13)
490. Not to eat of the meal offering brought by Aaron and his sons (Lev.6:16)

491. To observe the procedure of the sin-offering (Lev. 6:18)

492. Not to eat of the flesh of sin offerings, the blood of which is brought within the Sanctuary and sprinkled towards the Veil (Lev. 6:23)

493. To observe the procedure of the guilt-offering (Lev. 7:1)

494. To observe the procedure of the peace-offering (Lev. 7:11)

495. To burn meat of the holy sacrifice that has remained over (Lev.7:17)

496. Not to eat of sacrifices that are eaten beyond the appointed time for eating them (Lev. 7:18)

497. Not to eat of holy things that have become unclean (Lev. 7:19)

498. To burn meat of the holy sacrifice that has become unclean (Lev. 7:19

499. That a person who is unclean shall not eat of things that are holy (Lev. 7:20)

500. A Priest's daughter who profaned herself shall not eat of the holy things, neither of the heave offering nor of the breast, nor of the shoulder of peace offerings (Lev. 10:14, Lev. 22:12)

501. That a woman after childbirth shall bring an offering when she is clean (Lev. 12:6)

502. That the leper shall bring a sacrifice after he is cleansed (Lev.14:10)

503. That a man having an issue shall bring a sacrifice after he is cleansed of his issue (Lev. 15:13-15)

504. That a woman having an issue shall bring a sacrifice after she is cleansed of her issue (Lev. 15:28-30)

505. To observe, on Yom Kippur, the service appointed for that day, regarding the sacrifice, confessions, sending away of the scapegoat, etc. (Lev. 16:3-34)

506. Not to slaughter beasts set apart for sacrifices outside (Lev. 17:3-4)

507. Not to eat flesh of a sacrifice that has been left over (beyond the time appointed for its consumption) (Lev. 19:8)

508. Not to sanctify blemished cattle for sacrifice on the altar (Lev.22:20) This text prohibits such beasts being set apart for sacrifice on the altar

509. That every animal offered up shall be without blemish (Lev.22:21)

510. Not to inflict a blemish on cattle set apart for sacrifice (Lev.22:21)

511. Not to slaughter blemished cattle as sacrifices (Lev. 22:22)

512. Not to burn the limbs of blemished cattle upon the altar (Lev.22:22)

513. Not to sprinkle the blood of blemished cattle upon the altar (Lev. 22:24)

514. Not to offer up a blemished beast that comes from non-Israelites (Lev. 22:25)

515. That sacrifices of cattle can only take place when they are at least eight days old (Lev. 22:27)

516. Not to leave any flesh of the thanksgiving offering until the morning (Lev. 22:30)

517. To offer up the meal-offering of the Omer on the morrow after the first day of Passover, together with one lamb (Lev. 23:10)

518. Not to eat bread made of new grain before the Omer of barley has been offered up on the second day of Passover (Lev.23:14)

519. Not to eat roasted grain of the new produce before that time (Lev. 23:14)

520. Not to eat fresh ears of the new grain before that time (Lev.23:14)

521. To bring on wave loaves of bread together with the sacrifices which are then offered up in connection with the loaves [Pentecost feast] (Lev. 23:17-20)

522. To offer up an additional sacrifice on Passover (Lev. 23:36)

523. That one who vows to the Lord the monetary value of a person shall pay the amount appointed in the Scriptural portion (Lev.27:2-8)

524. If a beast is exchanged for one that had been set apart as an offering, both become sacred (Lev. 27:10)

525. Not to exchange a beast set aside for sacrifice (Lev. 27:10)

526. That one who vows to the Lord the monetary value of an unclean beast shall pay its value (Lev. 27:11-13)

527. That one who vows the value of a his house shall pay according to the appraisal of the Priest (Lev. 27:11-13)

528. That one who sanctifies to the Lord a portion of his field shall pay according to the estimation appointed in the Scriptural portion (Lev. 27:16-24)

529. Not to transfer a beast set apart for sacrifice from one class of sacrifices to another (Lev. 27:26)

530. To decide in regard to dedicated property as to which is sacred to the Lord and which belongs to the Priest (Lev. 27:28)

531. Not to sell a field devoted to the Lord (Lev. 27:28)

532. Not to redeem a field devoted to the Lord (Lev. 27:28)

533. To make confession before the Lord of any sin that one has committed, when bringing a sacrifice and at other times (Num.5:6-7)

534. Not to put olive oil in the meal-offering of a woman suspected of adultery (Num. 5:15)

535. Not to put frankincense on it (Num. 5:15)

536. 536.To offer up the regular sacrifices daily (two lambs as burnt offerings) (Num. 28:3)

537. To offer up an additional sacrifice every Sabbath (two lambs) (Num. 28:9)

538. To offer up an additional sacrifice every New Moon (Num. 28:11)

539. To bring an additional offering on the day of the first fruits (Num. 28:26-27)

540. To offer up an additional sacrifice on Rosh Hashanah (Num.29:1-6)

541. To offer up an additional sacrifice on the day of Atonement or Yom Kippur (Num. 29:7-8)

542. To offer up an additional sacrifice on Feast of Tabernacles (Num. 29:12-34)

543. To offer up an additional offering on the eighth day after the feast of Tabernacles, which is a festival by itself (Num. 29:35-38)

544. To bring all offerings, whether obligatory or freewill, on the first festival after these were incurred (Deut. 12:5-6)

545. Not to offer up sacrifices outside the Sanctuary (Deut. 12:13)

546. To offer all sacrifices in the Sanctuary (Deut. 12:14)

547. To redeem cattle set apart for sacrifices that contracted disqualifying blemishes, after which they may be eaten by anyone. (Deut. 12:15)

548. Not to eat of the unblemished firstling outside Jerusalem (Deut.12:17)

549. Not to eat the flesh of the burnt-offering (Deut. 12:17).

550. That the sons of Aaron shall not eat the flesh of the sin-offering or guilt-offering outside the Courtyard of the Sanctuary (Deut.12:17)

551. Not to eat of the flesh of the sacrifices that are holy in a minor degree, before the blood has been sprinkled on the altar (Deut. 12:17)

552. That the Priest shall not eat the first-fruits before they are set down in the Courtyard of the Sanctuary (Deut. 12:17)

553. To take trouble to bring sacrifices to the Sanctuary from places outside the land of Israel (Deut. 12:26)

554. Not to eat the flesh of beasts set apart as sacrifices, that have been rendered unfit to be offered up by deliberately inflicted blemish (Deut. 14:3)

555. Not to do work with cattle set apart for sacrifice (Deut. 15:19)

556. Not to shear beasts set apart for sacrifice (Deut. 15:19)

557. Not to leave any portion of the festival offering brought on the fourteenth of Nissan unto the third day (Deut. 16:4)

558. Not to offer up a beast that has a temporary blemish (Deut.17:1)

559. Not to bring sacrifices out of the hire of a harlot or price of a dog (Deut. 23:19)

560. To read the portion prescribed on bringing the first fruits (Deut.26:5-10)

REGARDING LAWS ABOUT RITUAL PURITY AND IMPURITY

561. That eight species of creeping things defile by contact (Lev.11:29-30)

562. That foods become defiled by contact with unclean things (Lev.11:34)

563. That anyone who touches the carcass of a beast that died of itself shall be unclean (Lev. 11:39)

564. That a lying-in woman is unclean like a menstruating woman (Lev. 12:2-5)

565. That a leper is unclean and defiles (Lev. 13:2-46)

566. That the leper shall be universally recognized as such by the prescribed marks So too, all other unclean persons should declare themselves as such (Lev. 13:45)

567. That a leprous garment is unclean and defiles (Lev. 13:47-49)

568. That a leprous house defiles (Lev. 14:34-46)

569. That a man, having a running issue, defiles (Lev. 15:1-15)
570. That the seed of copulation defiles (Lev. 15:16)
571. That purification from all kinds of defilement shall be effected by ceremonial washing (Lev. 15:16)
572. That a menstruating woman is unclean and defiles others (Lev.15:19-24)
573. That a woman, having a running issue, defiles (Lev. 15:25-27)
574. To carry out the ordinance of the Red Heifer so that its ashes will always be available (Num. 19:9)
575. That a corpse defiles (Num. 19:11-16)
576. That the waters of separation defile one who is clean, and cleanse the unclean from pollution by a dead body (Num.19:19-22)

REGARDING LAWS ABOUT LEPERS AND LEPROSY

577. Not to drove off the hair of the scalp (Lev. 13:33)
578. That the procedure of cleansing leprosy, whether of a man or of a house, takes place with cedar-wood, hyssop, scarlet thread, two birds, and running water (Lev. 14:1-7)
579. That the leper shall shave all his hair (Lev. 14:9)
580. Not to pluck out the marks of leprosy (Deut. 24:8)

REGARDING LAWS ABOUT THE KING

581. Not to curse a ruler, that is, the King in the land of Israel (Ex. 22:27)
582. To appoint a king (Deut. 17:15)
583. Not to appoint as ruler over Israel, one who comes from non-Israelites (Deut. 17:15)
584. That the King shall not acquire an excessive number of horses (Deut. 17:16)
585. That the King shall not take an excessive number of wives (Deut. 17:17)
586. That he shall not accumulate an excessive quantity of gold and silver (Deut. 17:17)
587. That the King shall write a scroll of the Torah for himself, in addition to the one that every person should write, so that he writes two scrolls (Deut. 17:18)

REGARDING LAWS ABOUT NAZARITES

588. That a Nazarite shall not drink wine, or anything mixed with wine which tastes like wine; and even if the wine or the mixture has turned sour, it is prohibited to him (Num. 6:3)
589. That he shall not eat fresh grapes (Num. 6:3)
590. That he shall not eat dried grapes (raisins) (Num. 6:3)
591. That he shall not eat the kernels of the grapes (Num. 6:4)
592. That he shall not eat of the skins of the grapes (Num. 6:4)

593. That the Nazarite shall permit his hair to grow (Num. 6:5)
594. That the Nazarite shall not cut his hair (Num. 6:5)
595. That he shall not enter any covered structure where there is a dead body (Num. 6:6)
596. That a Nazarite shall not defile himself for any dead person (by being in the presence of the corpse) (Num. 6:7)
597. That the Nazarite shall shave his hair when he brings his offerings at the completion of the period of his Nazariteship, or within that period if he has become defiled (Num. 6:9)

REGARDING LAWS GOVERNING WARS

598. That those engaged in warfare shall not fear their enemies nor be panic-stricken by them during battle (Deut. 3:22, 7:21,20:3)
599. To anoint a special Priest in a war (Deut. 20:2) This is today's equivalent to a military chaplain.
600. In a permissive war, to observe the procedure prescribed in the Torah (Deut. 20:10)
601. Not to keep alive any individual of the seven Canaanite nations (Deut. 20:16)
602. To exterminate the seven Canaanite nations from the land of Israel (Deut. 20:17)
603. Not to destroy fruit trees (Deut.20:19-20)
604. To deal with a beautiful woman taken captive in war in the manner prescribed in the Torah (Deut. 21:10-14)

605. Not to sell a beautiful woman (Deut.21:14)
606. Not to degrade a beautiful woman (taken captive in war) to the condition of a bondwoman (Deut. 21:14)
607. Not to offer peace to the Ammonites and the Moabites before waging war on them, as should be done to other nations (Deut.23:7)
608. That anyone who is unclean shall not enter the Camp of the Levites (Deut. 23:11)
609. To have a place outside the camp for sanitary purposes (Deut.23:13)
610. To keep that place sanitary (Deut. 23:14-15)
611. Always to remember what Amalek did (Deut. 25:17)
612. That the evil done to us by Amalek shall not be forgotten (Deut.25:19)
613. To destroy the seed of Amalek (Deut. 25:19)"
    (613 law of the Old Testament www.hisglory.us/ DOCUMENTS/613_biblical_lwas.htm)

Reading through the 613 Old Testament laws we can easily see that God clearly had a plan for mankind. He knew that we would need rules in order to live peaceably with one another. Through His leadership, He provided laws to His people that transcend any religious denomination or label. These laws were established in order that people would have possess some standard of mutual conduct, rules to live by, so that society would not fall into absolute chaos. The laws of the Old Testament show that we had, and indeed needed, rules of order. One need only take a view of the disorder in society today to witness what a departure from these laws results in.

As many nof our Founding Fathers were Christian believers and many were educated in seminaries, it is obvious, at least to me, that when our constitution was designed it was done so with the influence of biblical knowledge and that meant having laws to govern society by.

THE TEN COMMANDMENTS

These faulty, but honorable and dedicated humans saw the flaws in the original document and sought to correct them. Obviously, faults will occur with any manmade document, institution or operation. The desire to improve the original document is an example of how committed the Founders were to establishing a system of government that would serve all the people well into the future, "*to form a more perfect union…*". To this day, man continues to attempt to re-interpret the original meaning of our founding documents and its amendments. Even more dangerous is the attempts to re-interpret the meaning of the Scripture.

The Ten Commandments however, are laws handed down to Moses on Mt. Siani, from God, as a means of providing order to the Israelites. God also established laws that direct the interaction of people with God and each other and espouses certain punishment for violations.

The wandering tribe of Israel was in desperate need of rules to live by. They had fallen away from their worship and obedience to God's laws and had fallen away from the path God and set them on. They needed rules set forth to provide order and reminded them of what sin was until the promise of Christ was fulfilled. Not unlike our nation today that seems to reject the foundational laws that have established this as a nation of law and makes it possible to pursue your dream.

Consider the 10 Commandments. They are perfect in their construction and intent. The Constitution and amendments, while imminently better than any other in existence at the time and even today are not perfect. There is no ambiguity, nor is there a need to re-interpret the God's law. Although many today are putting great effort into doing just that. They mean what they mean! If one looks closely at the basic laws that govern our nation, it is evident that these laws have been derived from the explicit intent of conduct laid out in the 10 commandments and throughout the Bible.

1. ***Do not have other gods besides me (EX. 20:3 HCSB)***. To the Christian believer this seems straight forward. Simply put, it means that there is one God and only one God, regardless of what man may decide or choose to call Him. Those that trust in God are to have NO other. <u>No means no!</u> Even if you choose not to obey him. Deuteronomy 6:4,13-14 reinforces this, "*Listen Israel: The Lord our God, the Lord is One...Fear Yahweh your God, worship Him and take your oaths in His name. Do not follow other gods, the gods of the people around you*"(HCSB). He is still the one true and living God. Having many gods caused people

to shift their allegiances from one to the other as the situation dictates. Why is this a problem in America today? Because, as a nation we have fallen away from following the God that created this world and in effect created this nation as we know it. We have shifted away from following God in government, homes, schools, relationships and business. We have decided that God is a little god, not the God that create the universe. We have chosen to misinterpret His laws and we suffer for it. We have suffered from the loss of principle. When a nation adopts other gods like sports, fame, money, position, etc., it ceases to be a godly nation and will suffer. Look around our nation today, morality is laughed at, considered archaic and quite honestly is almost forgotten in some government circles. Hateful interaction is common place. The number of poor is on the rise, and the list goes on. As a nation we must acknowledge God and invite Him back into our world.

In a letter to a Mr. Warren, John Adams wrote about our new government, he said, *"This form of government is productive of everything which is great and excellent among men. But its principles are as easily destroyed, as human nature is corrupted. A government is only to be supported by pure religion or austere morals, Private, and public virtue is the only foundation of republics"*. (Warren–Adams letters, Boston MA Historical Society 1917).

2. **Do not make an idol for yourself (EX. HCSB).**
   This is a companion to the first. Once again no means no. Today were are surrounded by idols, human, things, places, money, etc. Our world is filled with idols of every shape and description. In our present time we live in a world that seeks "diols" that can accommodate to our latest whim and desire. One could make the case that our nation today is like a boat that has lost it mooring ties and is drifting on a dangerous, violent sea. Examine your community on any given Sunday. Are the churches full? Are the churches doing the work of the Lord or are they committed to other idols, recreation, home, business? Are churches motivated by the leading of Jesus or are they too busy competing with one another? One need not search long to discover some of the leading idols in society, sexual immorality, impurity, the worldly things. There was a time in our nation when business was permitted to be conducted on Sunday in allegiance to the "Sabbath day", so that God would be honored. Unfortunately those days were declared unconstitutional some years ago. Now we are "fortunate" enough to be able to shop, eat (and even buy alcohol) on the Lord's Day. Are we better off today than in those days gone by?

   Colossians 3:5,"Therefore, put to death what belongs to your worldly nature, sexual immorality, impurity, lust, evil desires, and greed, which is idolatry. Because of these God's wrath comes on the disobedient" (HCSB). Anytime something becomes more important than doing what God has called you to do, you have an idol. As previously stated, you can choose to do that, however there is a price for it.

3. **Do Not Misuse the name of the Lord our God"(EX.20:7 HCSB).** The command directs us not to take the Lord's name in vain. Neither should we use it flippantly. It is the Lord's name and not to be demeaned by carless and derogatory usage. Ezekiel 39:7 reads, *"So I will make My Holy name known among My people Israel and will no longer allow it to be profaned"* (HCSB). When God's name becomes something we say out of hat as just another adjective then we have stopped giving God the respect and fear due Him. Exodus 20:7 tells that God will not overlook the abuse of His name. "You shall not take the name of the Lord your God in vain, for the Lord will not hold him guiltless who takes his name in vain" (ESV).

4. **Remember the Sabbath Day to keep it Holy (EX.20:8 HCSB).** There was a time in society when virtually all businesses were closed on Sunday. I recall, as many also do, that cars were filled with gas on Saturday because no filling stations were open. Groceries were bought during the week as all grocery stores were closed on Sunday. Not to mention that where alcohol beverages were sold they were never sold on

Sunday, period. When we cheapen the name of the Lord we profane because we no longer find cause to honor it in our lives. When I look back I ask what kind of world would we have if we had not ventured away from keeping the Sabbath holy? Hebrews 10:29,"*How much worse punishment do you think one will deserve who has trampled on the Son of God, regarded as profane the blood of the covenant by which he has sanctified and insulted the Spirit of grace?*" (HCSB).

The previous four commandments discussed are instruction regarding our relationship to God. With these discarded, a society has only to spiral downward into a pit of lust and depravity that will overwhelm us. Our relationship with God is integral to our conduct as a civil society. Following God's law demands that we treat others with civility and fairness. While fairness is not always what one may wish, fairness under the law, God's and man's, is our obligation.

The following six Commandments address relationships with one another:

5. **"Honor your father and mother that your days may be in the land" Exodus 20:12 ESV).** When we disregard the four commandments mentioned above, we inevitably fail in the remaining six. Our society has become an environment where entertainment has subverted the role of parent/ adult by creating the impression that the adult is the lesser of the adult/child equation. Our society

has lessened the proper respect for the mother and father. We have suggested, quite adamantly in some quarters, that both are not required for a child to be reared in a healthy manner. We have adopted, through litigation, the attitude that one or the other is sufficient, in fact we even applaud those situations where there is the confusing status of two "fathers or "mothers". The need to honor the parents is paramount. When this has faded from a culture, those life lessons learned from hard work and acknowledgement of God's direction in their lives are not passed on and the culture for evermore changes, for the worse. This commandment is addressed in most every state law governing domestic relations. Domestic relations are often associated with husband/wife disputes or those that co-domicile with each other (meaning families), however most laws generally cover those that are or who previously resided in the same domicile.

6. **"You shall not murder" (Exodus 20:13 ESV).** We all can understand this commandment. It tells us that we are not to take a life with malice. This has been and will continue to be a very contentious point for those that misapply the meaning of this biblical law. The imposition of a penalty for a crime or the taking of life on the battlefield are not, in my opinion, with malice aforethought. Murder is a violation of civil law in every state of the union. The unjustified taking of a life is

clearly illegal as well as a violation of God's law. However, the argument is often made that God required his servants to completely annihilate His enemies at times. God was always justified in this requirement. In virtually every society current or passed, the wanton, malicious, premediated taking of a life is a violation on societal laws, norms and mores. Even in our own society today, we still hold this to be a most heinous crime.

7. **"You shall not commit adultery" (Exodus 20:14 ESV)**. God's word tells that we are not to commit adultery. We are not to engage in sexual relations outside the marriage bond. God demonstrates his omniscience in that He knows what damage adultery brings into a life. The scars it produces are often irrevocable. Adultery causes families to be divided, with children often being the brunt of the effect. Many times adultery and the resulting divorce are the catalyst for juvenile behavior that may result in criminal behavior as a sign of crying out because they know of no other way to express their hurt.

While compassion and God's mercy can heal a marriage, it will never be the same. In our present society, the act of adultery has been redefined as a victimless crime and many states have removed it from their criminal codes, thinking it is an act of adult discretion and therefore, at worst, a civil matter. Regardless of how society may currently view adultery, it is not "victimless". The damage that is causes to families is severe and often irreparable.

8. **"You shall not steal" (Exodus 20:16 ESV)**. To me this is an easy one. Stealing means taking anything (big or small, or great or little value), that does not belong to you or you do not have express permission to take. Pretty simple, don't steal! Theft, the taking of another's property or goods without the owner's permission is illegal in all 50 states. In both ancient and modern societies that do not possess the sophistication that we do in this country, stealing is frowned upon and often punished severely, sometimes by death. The taking of another's property, by any description is unacceptable and every state in this union has laws governing such acts.

9. **"You shall not bear false witness against your neighbor" (Exodus 20:16 ESV)**. A false witness is one that fabricates evidence and offers it up as testimony against someone when in fact, they have no real or relevant knowledge of the issue at hand. It's someone that seeks to harm another through falsehoods. In our society today it seems that we hear more fabricated "stories" about every issue. Even our news media has fallen into the trap of using fictional, unverified information to promote topics they have a particular affinity for. In short, this means lying is wrong! We see on an

almost daily basis, individuals being charged with false statements in connection to an investigation or some other type of official conduct. They go to great extremes to label this lying as something else so as not to be tainted with such a destructive title. The breakdown of a society where honesty is not a truly valued characteristic is a society in a downward spiral.

10. **10. "You shall not covet your neighbor's house, you shall not covert your neighbor's wife, or his man servant, or his female servant, or his ox, or his donkey, or anything that is your neighbor's" (Exodus 20:17 ESV)**. In a nut shell this is about keeping up with the Jones'. Trying to have more than the other guy! Our society tells us that the more stuff you have the better off you are. While, in my opinion, that may seem to be truthful, often the stuff becomes more of a burden than enjoyment, thus the massive growth in the yard sale market.

It occurs to me that too often we overlook the word "shall". "Keeping up with the Joneses" seems to be the order of the day for others, even it means putting all else aside. Falling into the trap of covetousness leads us to want more things. When "things" become our driving force we are easily drawn away from our guiding principles.

The 10 Commandments lay out a method of living that is intended to direct the individual onto a path of righteous living. The word "righteous" is often taken, in today's critical society, to mean perfection, or superior, or even elitist. In fact, it means to live by the Word of God a life determined to live by the principle that God established for all man-kind. God has directed us, in His commandments, to live for Him, then to live with one another. The first four commandments give us a pattern by which we may relate to Him. The remaining commandments tell us how we are to live with each other. While these particular commandments do not spell out every situation, one need not strain to find application in them for all of life.

LAWS IN AMERICA

In our country there are two basic types of laws, moral and civil. The moral laws are those given so that we can, and should, live in a decent society. One that does not honor vile or deviant behavior. The civil laws are given so that we might have a society with order and tells us how we are to interact with each other, they are the rules for social conduct. Rules such as paying what you owe, not stealing from or cheating others. We have laws that direct our domestic relations, when to pay taxes and so forth.

As you look back on the fundamental laws given to Moses by God, we see that that the moral laws, or as stated in the Constitution, laws of nature and nature's God, are given so that mankind might have a clear understanding of what proper behavior is between humans and the even all of creation. The 10 commandments tell us that certain wrongs ought never to be committed. Murder is easy to understand. Murder is different that killing. While many may argue this point I am convinced that when the Apostle Peter was told "kill and eat, call nothing unclean that I call clean", God established a clear line between the two. Murder is the willful taking of another's life with malice aforethought. Our present laws have deciphered that single command into many subparts, however the intent is the same, the taking of a life without cause for your personal gratification or benefit, is prohibited, no matter what man calls it.

In the Bible, God provided laws to govern man's conduct with one another, because He understood the nature of man. Man's nature will, more often than not, lead him to commit acts or do things that are in his best interest and often to the detriment of others. This is why we needs laws. This is why the Framers of our Constitution saw that the laws of a free nation must start with the original laws, the Ten Commandments.

"To say that religion is a big topic of interest to a lot of people in the United States today is a bit of an understatement. It would, however, be incorrect to say that because of the great deal of attention religion and government is getting today, it is a more important topic now than ever before. On the contrary, religion and government has been a matter of great importance and concern to many for centuries.

Today, some headlines highlight some of the issues that surround us: The Chief Justice of the Alabama Supreme Court is removed from office for refusing to remove a monument to the Ten Commandments from his court house building. A California atheist sues to remove the words "under God" from the <u>Pledge of Allegiance</u> and loses; then wins on appeal; then loses in the Supreme Court. President George W. Bush is criticized for his idea of the Faith-Based Initiative, where faith-based organizations could get federal funds where previously they had been barred. Public school bus drivers are required to remove holiday decorations from their buses after complaints of "offended" parents.

These stories, some national, some local, all have one thing in common — the relationship between religion and government. It is a sticky wicket. We are a nation of many religious faiths, and many of us work for a government in some capacity. Is there any way that religion, and the religiousness of people, can be separated from government and the role of people in government? Can religion and government co-exist without crossing over each other's boundaries? What are those boundaries? What exactly is the separation of church and state?

These are some of the questions that this topic page will address. Likely, this page will not change any one's mind on the subject. The goal is not to change minds, but to explain what is in the Constitution, what the Supreme Court has said about the topic over time, and how the topic is being seen today.

RELIGION IN THE
ORIGINAL CONSTITUTION

Religion makes only one direct and obvious appearance in the original Constitution that seems to point to a desire for some degree of religious freedom. That appearance is in <u>Article 6</u>, at the end of the third clause:

> *[N]o religious Test shall ever be required as a Qualification to any Office or public Trust under the United States.*

This statement is simple and straight-forward, and applies to all offices in the entire United States, both state and federal. The clause simply means that no public position can be required to be held by any one of any religious denomination. It would be unconstitutional for there to be a requirement that the President by Lutheran, or even for the mayor of a small town to be Christian. Likewise, it would be unconstitutional for a law to forbid a Jew or Muslim from holding any office in any governmental jurisdiction in the United States. (This having been said, it should be noted that <u>several state constitutions do have a religious test</u> — specifically, they deny office to anyone unwilling to acknowledge God or a Supreme Being.)

There is one other direct bow to religion in the original Constitution, and it is a bit obtuse. The Presidential Oath of Office is codified in the Constitution in this way:

> *I do solemnly swear (or affirm) that I will faithfully execute the Office of President of the United States, and will to the best of my Ability, preserve, protect and defend the Constitution of the United States.*

Finally, the Constitution refers to the year that the Convention created the document as "the Year of our Lord one thousand seven hundred and Eighty seven." Some have argued that the use of the term "Lord" in this way is indicative of something, but it is indicative of nothing more than a standard way of referring to years in that time period. Some state constitutions are not shy about referencing God.

THE FIRST AMENDMENT

The Framers thought that they had constructed a very complete and comprehensive document. But many people disagreed, and though the opposition had many issues with the Constitution, they focused on one in particular: the lack of a bill of rights.

> *"The civil rights of none shall be abridged on account of religious belief or worship, nor shall any national religion be established, nor shall the full and equal rights of conscience be in any manner, or on any pretext, infringed."*

Through the debates in the House, Senate, and conference committees, the wording of all of the proposed amendments was whittled down to the religion clauses of what is our 1st Amendment:

> *Congress shall make no law respecting an establishment of religion, or prohibiting the free exercise thereof.*

Does this final version have the same effect of all the other proposals? Whereas in Europe, the "establishment of religion" did mean a state church, it took on a whole new meaning in America. Several attempts were made in several states to have and maintain official churches, but the multitude of denominations made it increasingly difficult to do so. If a state established the Congregationalist Church and required taxes be paid to it, it was not long before Lutherans or Baptists began to refuse to pay the tax. By the time the Constitution was ratified, several states had official state churches, but not official state denominations. In other words, a state would charter a church as it would a business today, but it would have no other formal role in the running of the church. Even that practice was waning, with only six states incorporating churches in any way by 1789. Clearly, the trend in church/state relations was towards no relationship at all.

In the end, the 1st Amendment not only prevents the establishment of a national religion, but it also prohibits government aid to any religion, even on an non-preferential basis, as well as protecting the right of the individual to choose to worship, or not, as he or she sees fit.

The Wall of Separation

Often when someone speaks of the constitutionally guaranteed right to religion, they also speak of "the wall of separation between church and state," or simply as "the separation of church and state." What does this mean, and what is the origin of this phrase?

It did not take long after the passage and ratification of the 1ˢᵗ Amendment for people to start interpreting it to simply mean that that federal government had no business getting mixed into religion. Of course, there is more to it than that, especially when it comes to the individual right part of the amendment. But the notion that the government should not become enmeshed in religion is an important concept, too. There is nothing in the Constitution that specifically says that there is a wall of separation between religion and government. The Wall, however, is a nice shorthand metaphor for non-establishment.

Thomas Jefferson, in his <u>1802 letter to the Danbury Baptist Association</u>, then-President Jefferson used the phrase — it was probably not the first time, but it is the most memorable one. He said:

Believing with you that religion is a matter which lies solely between man and his god, [the people, in the 1ˢᵗ Amendment,] declared that their legislature should make no law respecting an establishment of religion, or prohibiting the free exercise thereof, thus building a wall of separation between church and state.

Jefferson, an outspoken proponent of the separation of church and state, drafted a bill that was designed to quash an attempt by some to provide taxes for the purpose of furthering religious education. He wrote that such support for religion was counter to a natural right of man:... *no man shall be compelled to frequent or support any religious worship, place, or ministry whatsoever, nor shall be enforced, restrained, molested, or burthened in his body or goods, nor shall otherwise suffer, on account of his religious opinions or belief; but that all men shall be free to profess, and by argument to maintain, their opinions in matters of religion, and that the same shall in no wise diminish, enlarge, or affect their civil capacities. Excerpted from the web site https://usconstitution.net and is intended to provide background about the Bill of Rights and the disputes that surrounded them regarding religion:*

THE PLEDGE OF ALLEGIANCE

In 2000, Dr. Michael Newdow filed suit in United States District Court, suing the United States Congress, the President of the United States, the State of California, and the Elk Grove Unified School District. The suit was filed by Newdow on the behalf of his daughter, who was a kindergarten student in the Elk Grove District at the time. The suit alleged that the school policy that the Pledge of Allegiance by recited by students was a violation of his daughter's religious freedom because of the inclusion of the words "under God" in the Pledge. In his complaint, Newdow noted that he was an atheist and opposed to the use of the words in the Pledge. Without the words "under God," Newdow was not opposed to the Pledge.

The District Court ruled on the case on June 26, 2002. The panel of three judges split on the decision, 2-1, but found for Newdow. The public furor over the decision was swift, with people from the President to top members of Congress calling the decision "out of the mainstream" and "stupid." The District Court found that the Pledge, in its current form (the words "under God" were added in 1954), did not pass the Lemon Test:

> In the context of the Pledge, the statement that the United States is a nation "under God" is an endorsement of religion. It is a profession of a religious belief, namely, a belief in monotheism. The recitation that ours is a nation "under God" is not a mere acknowledgment that many Americans believe in a deity. Nor is it merely descriptive of the undeniable historical significance of religion in the founding of the Republic. Rather, the phrase "one nation under God" in the context of the Pledge is normative. To recite the Pledge is not to describe the United States; instead, it is to swear allegiance to the values for which the flag stands: unity, indivisibility, liberty, justice, and — since 1954 — monotheism. The text of the official Pledge, codified in federal law, impermissibly takes a position with respect to the purely religious question of the existence and identity of God. A profession that we are a nation "under God" is identical, for Establishment Clause purposes, to a profession that we are a nation "under Jesus," a nation "under Vishnu," a nation under Zeus," or a nation "under no god," because none of these professions can be neutral with respect to religion.

The Supreme Court ended up ducking the question, restoring the status quo until another challenge is issued.

,("Origins of the Bill of Rights", by Leonard Levy, (Yale University Press, New Haven CT, 1999),(Steve Mount, "Constitutional Topic: The Constitution and Religion", (hhtps://usconstitution.net/consttop_rel. html#original, 2017), "The Bill of Rights, by Akhill Amar (Yale University Press, New Haven,CT, 1998))

So, Why Do We Need the Law?

Almost everything we do is governed by some set of rules. There are rules for games, for social clubs, for sports and for adults in the workplace. There are also rules imposed by morality and custom that play an important role in telling us what we should and should not do. However, some rules -- those made by the state or the courts -- are called "laws". Laws resemble morality because they are designed to control or alter our behavior. But unlike rules of morality, laws are enforced by the courts; if you break a law -- whether you like that law or not -- you may be forced to pay a fine, pay damages, or go to prison.

Why are some rules so special that they are made into laws? Why do we need rules that **everyone** must obey? In short, what is the purpose of law?

If we did not live in a structured society with other people, laws would not be necessary. We would simply do as we please, with little regard for others. But ever since individuals began to associate with other people -- to live in society --laws have been the glue that has kept society together. For example, the law in Canada states that we must drive our cars on the right-hand side of a two-way street. If people were allowed to choose at random which side of the street to drive on, driving would be dangerous and chaotic. Laws regulating our business affairs help to ensure that people keep their promises. Laws against criminal conduct help to safeguard our personal property and our lives.

Even in a well-ordered society, people have disagreements and conflicts arise. The law must provide a way to resolve these disputes peacefully. If two people claim to own the same piece of property, we do not want the matter settled by a duel: we turn to the law and to institutions like the courts to decide who the real owner is and to make sure that the real owner's rights are respected.

We need law, then, to ensure a safe and peaceful society in which individuals' rights are respected. But we expect even more from our law. Some totalitarian governments have cruel and arbitrary laws, enforced by police forces free to arrest and punish people without trial. Strong-arm tactics may provide a great deal of order, but we reject this form of control.

The Canadian legal system respects individual rights while, at the same time, ensuring that society operates in an orderly manner. In Canada, we also believe in the Rule of Law, which means that the law applies to every person, including members of the police and other public officials, who must carry out their public duties in accordance with the law.

GOALS OF LAWS

In our society, laws are not only designed to govern our conduct: they are also intended to give effect to social policies. For example, some laws provide for benefits when workers are injured on the job, for health care, as well as for loans to students who otherwise might not be able to go to university.

Another goal of the law is fairness. This means that the law should recognize and protect certain basic individual rights and freedoms, such as liberty and equality. The law also serves to ensure that strong groups and individuals do not use their powerful positions in society to take unfair advantage of weaker individuals.

However, despite the best intentions, laws are sometimes created that people later recognize as being unjust or unfair. In a democratic society like Canada, laws are not carved in stone, but must reflect the changing needs of society. In a democracy, anyone who feels that a particular law is flawed has the right to speak out publicly and to seek to change the law by lawful means.

THE SYSTEM OF LAW AND JUSTICE

The law is a set of rules for society, designed to protect basic rights and freedoms, and to treat everyone fairly. These rules can be divided into two basic categories: public law and private law.

PUBLIC LAW

Public law deals with matters that affect society as a whole. It includes areas of the law that are known as criminal, constitutional and administrative law. These are the laws that deal with the relationship between the individual and the state, or among jurisdictions. For example, if someone breaks a criminal law, it is regarded as a wrong against society as a whole, and the state takes steps to prosecute the offender. *(http://www.oas.org/jurisdico/mla/en/can/en_can_mla_what.html)*

Private Law

Private law, on the other hand, deals with the relationships between individuals in society and is used primarily to settle private disputes. Private law deals with such matters as contracts, property ownership, the rights and obligations of family members, and damage to one's person or property caused by others. When one individual sues another over some private dispute, this is a matter for private law. Private suits are also called "civil" suits.

As you can easily surmise, the laws of the Old Testament were contained in the original 10, with additions added for nearly every societal situation that could have occurred in the days of the ancients. The 613 laws previously stated cover every aspect of human relations, domestic, business, judicial, war, and many social issues that today are debated as to their need or appropriateness in a modern society.

To gain a full comprehension of where and how our laws came into being, we must return to the Founders of this nation. Men, such as Thomas Jefferson who penned the Declaration of Independence, were more likely thinking in the deist realm when the Declaration of Independence and the Constitution were drafted. While many were religious men of the time, they sought to create a nation based on laws that included all faiths, and prevented the government from requiring any specific belief, or none at all. Jefferson wrote the following: *in proof that they meant to comprehend, within the mantle of its protection, the Jew and the Gentile, the Christian and Muslim, the Hindu and Infidel of every denomination."* (Thomas Jefferson, Autobiography, in reference to his Virginia Act for Religious Freedom, 1743-1826, http://christianity.thoughts.com)

Mind you, Thomas Jefferson wrote: *"Of all the systems of morality, ancient or modern, which have come under my observation, none appear to me so pure as that of Jesus."*

(Thomas Jefferson, Autobiography, in reference to his Virginia Act for Religious Freedom, 1743-1826, http://christianity.thoughts.com)

Even in the Garden of Eden, God saw that man would be unable to conduct himself in accordance with God's commends, so he instituted laws, laws governing nature and man. When Cain slew Able, he paid a heavy price, outcast from his family and bearing the mark of conviction. Even so today, we look to minimize or obviate our laws to suit our actions. Our laws are here to keep us civil and living in harmony with one another. When we violate these laws, we stand in jeopardy of the consequences under the judicial system. This system was intended to be fair and equitable to every person regardless of station in life. However, because of our lust for self-satisfaction, we have altered our system and bent its function toward those with financial, or political means.

We live in a nation founded on the principle of laws (their origin discussed previously). There is not a government on this land that does not need and use laws to ensure that it is serving it's anointed purpose. Government, and their laws, are designed to protect us from ourselves and consequently others. How sad it would be if the final legacy of our nation was to be that we failed to honor a system that was the shining example to the world of juris prudence with equality.

SUBMISSION TO AUTHORITIES

Let every person be subject to the governing authorities. For there is no authority except from God, and those that exist have been instituted by God. Therefore whoever resists the authorities resists what God has appointed, and those who resist will incur judgment. For rulers are not a terror to good conduct, but too bad. Would you have no fear of the one who is in authority? Then do what is good, and you will receive his approval, for he is God's servant for your good. But if you do wrong, be afraid, for he does not bear the sword in vain. For he is the servant of God, an avenger who carries out God's wrath on the wrongdoer. Therefore one must be in subjection, not only to avoid God's wrath but also for the sake of conscience."(Romans 13:1-5 English Standard Version (ESV)

Finally, you have to determine for yourself if you believe that our Founders were acting on their belief and under the inspiration of Godly influence when they established this nation and constructed our Constitution. You, the individual must determine for yourself if you believe that our Founders were men of faith or not. You must determine through your own investigation if you stand on the side of a Divine leading in the establishment of our nation or simply an act of intelligent and enlightened men that "happened" to get it right!

Think on this. How coincidental is it that people, under the hand of a tyrannical ruler thousands of miles away, would be able to stand against an imperial military that virtually ruled the world and defeat it with an army of farmers, teacher, lawyers and preachers? It think it possible would require more than simple human desire. There must have been a greater influence in those that chose to commit this act of treason against the crown. I am of the belief that it was an act of divine leading. If so, then the establishment would have also been an act of divine leadership. For my part I will stand with Divine intervention.

In our present society we have a constant struggle about the application of religious belief in the administration of our laws. This argument will persist long after this present generation has passed from existence. It has often been said by others that I would rather be ruled by an incompetent that strives to live by God's principles than to be dominated by a one that appears to know how but relies on the world's definitions of right and wrong.

To fully understand the foundation of our nation one must see clearly where our Founders gained their inspiration. As I said previously, although these were men that possessed many faults, as all humans do, their intent was to act upon the guidance they firmly believed was of a Divine nature. Forgetting from whence this nation was birthed, will lead us into an abyss of moral decay that may not be recoverable.

I trust this book will lead you to dig deeper into the origins of our laws and how, or if, they are related to scriptural laws handed down from on high. *(Agel, Jerome B. We The People-Great Documents of the American Nation, New York, NY: Barnes & Noble Books, 2000; Amar, Akhil Reed, American Constitution-A Biography, New Yory, NY: Random House, 2005; Amar, Akhil Reed, The Bill of Rights-Creation and Reconstruction, New Haven, CT: Yale University Press, 1998)*

If nothing I have said previously make you think on this issue, then allow me to leave you with one final thought to consider:

ROMANS 13: 1-7 (KJV)

Let every soul be subject unto the higher powers. For there is no power but of God: the powers that be are ordained of God.

Whosoever therefore resisteth the power, resisteth the ordinance of God: and they that resist shall receive to themselves damnation.

For rulers are not a terror to good works, but to the evil. Wilt thou then not be afraid of the power? do that which is good, and thou shalt have praise of the same:

For he is the minister of God to thee for good. But if thou do that which is evil, be afraid; for he beareth not the sword in vain: for he is the minister of God, a revenger to [execute] wrath upon him that doeth evil.

Wherefore [ye] must needs be subject, not only for wrath, but also for conscience sake.

For for this cause pay ye tribute also: for they are God's ministers, attending continually upon this very thing.

Render therefore to all their dues: tribute to whom tribute [is due]; custom to whom custom; fear to whom fear; honor to whom honor.

Printed in the United States
By Bookmasters